What Men Don't Know About Sex...
That Women Could Teach Them

Chuck Spezzano, Ph.D.

 Psychology *of* Vision

First published in the UK July 2011 by MyVoice Publishing

Edited by Eric Taylor
Cover design by Lizzie Prior
book publishing commissioned by Psychology of Vision UK & Ireland with special thanks to Anna Baldwin

www.psychologyofvision.co.uk

Published by: MyVoice Publishing,
Unit 1,
16 Maple Road,
Eastbourne,
BN23 6NY

ISBN: 978-0-9554692-9-9

Dedication

For Julie Wookey,
our great friend and fellow pioneer.
What a gal!

Acknowledgments

I would like to acknowledge the team at our office Charlie, Shawna, Kenny and Harrylyn.

Sunny was invaluable in supporting this book to completion.

I'd also like to mention my family, Lency, Chris and J'aime for their continual inspiration.

God Bless You All!

And finally *A Course in Miracles* for its inestimable influence in my life.

Contents

Introduction

Welcome to a book about a subject that many like to talk about, and most like to experience first hand. While exceptions prove the rule, let me unabashedly state that this is a book of generalizations. And as Oscar Wilde once stated, "Every generalization is untrue, including this one."

There is an elegance to the love and intimacy in relationships that can take us beyond the human realm and open us up to the Divine. The men who know about this do not have to be educated, just joined with at ever higher and deeper levels. But, then there are most men, and this book is about them.

I have always been keenly interested in the subject of sex. Hands down, it was my favourite subject. OK, maybe my hands weren't down when it came to sex. When I was a kid, I had such a gift in catching frogs in the creek behind our house that I got to be known as "the fastest hands in Rockdale." This was to prove helpful later when I commenced dating.

I love sex as much as the next man. OK, maybe even more than the next man, because I'm Italian. When I was a kid I enjoyed playing doctor so much I became one when I got older. My wife and I have been married over 23 years. After our first year of marriage, she said the only thing she didn't understand about me was why I had gone into psychology instead of gynaecology. I tried to explain the difference between that which I loved and felt called to do as my life's work, and what I just plain loved. She simply smiled in a knowing way. She does that a lot with me.

In the first workshop that my wife and I taught in Frankfurt, Germany, our interpreter and now close friend, Monica Casey, got stumped over something I said. My wife, in an aside to her, said, "If you ever don't know what Chuck is talking about, just assume it has a sexual reference." Then with that knowing smile she continued, "He can't help it; he's Italian."

Furthermore, I'm a guy. I look out at the world with three eyes. A guy's view of the world is limited. It's like he's in a submarine. He doesn't realize that looking at the world through his "periscope" does not give him the "*whole*" perspective. And as we all know: "Women are from Venus. Men are from Penis."

Sacred Irreverence

Ladies, if you haven't already guessed it, I am approaching this most delicate of subjects with a "sacred irreverence." I have found that this approach allows me to go into the deepest level of suffering with someone who has experienced trauma, but with a note of lightness that keeps us from getting bogged down in pain, blame, guilt or shame. I use this same element of lightness when approaching relationships, especially classic man/woman relationships. The light approach allows men to deal with subjects in a way that is neither mystifying nor emotionally overwhelming.

I have also found that anyone who has a sexual issue, whether buried or conscious, reacts to my style. Then, if they don't become overly judgmental right away and give up the chance at any possibility of healing, it allows me to spot those who need help and respond to them. Recognizing and acknowledging the problem is more than half the battle in regaining a wholesome, balanced sex life.

The final benefit of such a light approach is that you can get and keep a man's attention with the use of humour. It is one of the few ways that a man will allow you to educate him. So if you have not been employing humour it is likely that your man will not feel grateful about what you teach him, no matter how vital the education seems or how well you present it. How funny you make something will be much more important than what you want to communicate. You may find yourself challenged as you go to educate your man about sex, because almost every man thinks of himself as a "stud muffin," God's gift to women. This book is meant to make that less of a challenge.

Of course, you know the other way to get a man's attention. It's the same reason why women wear T-shirts that read: "These are not my eyes!" On the other hand, some men have taken to wearing their counterpart: "Tell your boobs to stop staring at my eyes!!!" When you shake "the girls", you get "the boys'" attention. If you beam energy out of them, men become like deer caught in the headlights.

How to Make Your Man Feel Loved

At the beginning of a relationship, a couple relates to each other on many levels. As the relationship moves on, the partners in a couple relate to each other in *their* own favourite way, which is not necessarily their partner's favourite way. I knew a couple where both husband and wife complained they felt unloved. The husband ran two companies, came home, cleaned the house and took care of their toddler to give his wife a break. He almost fell off his chair when his wife claimed he didn't love her.

"How can you say that? Look at all I do for you!" he admonished. The husband was obviously a "visual" type of personality. He liked presents, a good presentation, a clean house and an attractive partner. He liked to be shown that he was loved by having things done for him. And as a visual, he did so love to peek.

His wife said her husband didn't love her because he never *told* her he loved her. She was obviously an "auditory" type. She had the biggest hurt look in her eyes when her husband recounted that she didn't love him.
"How can you say that?" she asked. "I'm *always* telling you I love you." A partner like this loves to hear you say you love him in a sexy or loving tone of voice, and wants you to talk suggestively to him. Phone sex appeals to auditory types.

The other type of partner is a "kinaesthetic," or a "feeler." If you don't touch a kinaesthetic, he doesn't feel loved. Learn what your partner likes to be given by what he gives to you. If you give on all three levels, you will probably have a happy partner. Your partner may relate through all three categories, or simply one or two. Find out how he likes to be shown love, and teach him how you really know when you are loved. If you spell things out without seeming to, you have become a master educator.

Foreplay

Couples grow into habits regarding sex, which can make your relationship feel old, and your sex life stale. Your man must be trained in how *you* like sex and taught the ways in which you are not like him. Teach him how to slow down and take his time. This is a generous act on his part, which he will likely do out of his love for you. It is good not to try to accomplish this through controlling him because that will just build resentment. Let him know when he's doing it right. Be demonstrative and full of praise. Talk to him about how you like sex. You could say, for example, "It's soooo good when you do . . .." Your man feels great when you feel great about sex. Educate him without seeming to. Don't make it a big deal. Use his natural desire to please you as leverage. You can ask your higher mind about how to accomplish this and wait for inspiration. It will come to you if you are not frightened or in a fight.

For couples who are caught in old habits regarding sex, what I usually prescribe is a week of "Girl's Treat." This means anytime, anywhere and any way *you* want it. Or you can have a week off from sex if that is your desire. Your partner is to totally surrender to you. This is when you can teach him how fun your way is. The next week is "Boy's Treat," when he gets his preferences in regard to frequency, position, etc. He can be enthusiastic about your week because he knows his week is coming. I usually suggest a minimum of three rounds for each. When done with willingness, this exercise can revive a lagging sex life.

In your everyday life, when you are not in the mood, don't have a lot of time or energy, or have other things on your mind, you can give your partner Boy's Treat. This is giving him play time with you sexually where he can do it however he wants it (within certain limits if you insist). You are giving him a sign that you love him without him necessarily expecting you to come up with an orgasm yourself. "Boy's Treat" will make him happy if you show up for the short time necessary to be in service to him. It doesn't take much for him to feel you love him. In the same way, you can teach him it's not all about sex, in spite of what "Mr. Lucky" tells him. Teach him about romance by bringing romance in. If he doesn't have the temperament or natural skill for romance, teach him about it. He probably had no role models for it when he was growing up. If you join him in sex for a short tryst, you can then proceed to show him other great ways of being together. If sex is the last thing you feel like doing, rather than feeling in sacrifice, think of joining him sexually as a way of giving to him and loving him. In the same way, you can show him how to be in service to you in a loving way when he is not in the mood. This will save lots of time and problems in the long run. Don't keep your man in the doghouse, throwing him a bone every once in a while. This level of control and competition reflects poorly on both of you and allows your fear to rule the relationship.

Your man doesn't necessarily realize that each woman is unique in what turns her on. So besides teaching him about sex, you must also teach him what works for *you* in sex. Men don't even realize that the reason most women fake orgasm is because most men fake foreplay.

My wife spent twenty-one years making me an expert on foreplay to the point where I loved foreplay. Girl's Treat became my favourite way also. But then after I had mastered foreplay and looked forward to it as great fun, she told me, "Foreplay, shmoreplay. Climb aboard!" When I had come to the point of totally valuing foreplay, she felt it was overrated. This was a couple of years after we had reached a level where, in five to ten minutes, we had *totally* and wonderfully satisfied each other. We felt kind of smug about it, like a veteran couple with veteran couplings. This stage eventually gave way to other stages and the adventure continued.

In every country I've taught in, I have heard women tell their men to "slow down" in regard to sex. This is the general rule. Though again, after I'd mastered "super slow," my wife wanted me to be "super fly" again, like I was at the beginning of the relationship. And, of course, some women do prefer it "faster and faster."

Remember that Heaven will help you to help him, and also help your relationship through guidance and inspiration. This will not only make you happy; it will help you to remember that awakening to love, God and Oneness is where you can experience the Big 'O.' The greater the intimacy, the greater the satisfaction and the joy. Men who don't know this think of sex in terms of quantity rather than quality because almost all sex has quality for them. Men usually think in terms of "the more the better." This is especially true when they are young and their sexual energy is strong, especially when a relationship is first beginning. This is when they most often confuse sex with "drilling for oil."

Many young wives are distressed by the fact that as soon as they so much as smile at their partner, he wants to jump her. This can be quite off-putting for the wife and it is likely that she will pull away—which can be quite off-putting for the husband.

To be able to help guide, direct and focus a man's sexual energy, you must be comfortable with your own sexuality. If you are not, or have been wounded in some way, keep committing to your success in sex and your success with your partner, so that it does not become a "bone" of contention that separates you. What I can tell you from all my years of personal and professional experience is this. If you have been wounded in sex, you were actually already naturally gifted in sexuality, but took on an injury to disguise it. One of the easiest ways to uncover this gift is to keep committing to sex, to yourself as a sexual partner and to your sexual partnership with your man. The power of commitment, which is to choose to give yourself fully, takes you and your relationship to the next stage of having loving sex. Commitment is one of the most powerful healing tools in a relationship.

If you are comfortable with your own sexuality, you will be comfortable with his. You can then demonstrate that the feeling aspect of sex is not an obstacle he has to get through until he gets what he wants, but is the "juice" that adds depth and richness. Likewise, you can show him the spiritual connection that can take place in sex through the depth of intimacy. The more joining that takes place, the more grace is natural to your lovemaking. Trying to talk to him about this is usually unsuccessful, but sharing it with him in a loving way is quite effective.

Touching

Ladies, teach your men the value of foreplay. And men, if you spend long minutes touching your wife, simply for the sake of loving her, without rushing into any erogenous zones, you will build a deep and lasting sex life with your wife that can go on long after most couples have "petered" out.

When a couple has run out of sexual steam, I have typically prescribed a two-week timeout in regard to sex. For that period of time sex is off-limits. On the other hand, I instruct them to touch each other at least thirty minutes a day. Sometimes thirty minutes each. It could even be an hour for each of them, but they are not to touch any explicit erogenous zones, such as genitals, nipples, etc. This can reverse the sexual deadness in a relationship. Touching is a great aphrodisiac and it really confirms your partner. Prolonged touching bonds you at ever deeper levels and keeps your love and sexual relationship unfolding, even into your golden years. Use your touch as a vehicle for communicating love, and it will have a salutary effect on your sex life.

Now, ladies, know that when your man comes over to hold, help or comfort you, he does so sheerly out of love, generously reaching out to you as his beloved. But after holding you for ten to twenty minutes, he gets another thought: What could be even better than this? And what do you think his little head comes up with?

He didn't come over to you with the ulterior motive of sex in mind, but given some minutes of intimacy these thoughts do arise. Soon you are feeling the familiar tap on your leg of his "one-eyed trouser snake" about to become a "heat-seeking moisture missile." Forgive him. It wasn't his first thought, but it's definitely his last one. The reason a man is said to think too much is because he has two heads. It is also why a woman is said to talk too much. She has two mouths.

Teach your man the happy power of touching. It will soothe and relax you, and make you quite responsive to his ministrations, so everyone wins.

Sex in Context

To truly speak about sex, it must be done in the context of relationship. A woman's response to this information is, "Duh!" A guy's response to this is, "Really, how come? I thought it was 'any port in a storm.'"

A woman knows that if your relationship is in trouble, the sex will be also. These same principles are true in both man/woman and in gay relationships, but in gay relationships the masculine/feminine aspects can be much more fluid, and passed back and forth—sometimes quite quickly.

In the Beginning

In the beginning of a relationship, both partners are generally happy with the amount of sex and its quality, but many times that does not last. As the relationship wears on, especially after marriage, other factors can enter the picture. I have known a number of people who were practicing celibacy. Unfortunately, most of them were married. Besides the novelty wearing off, other factors that hitherto were eclipsed by love, romance and the binding force of sex can affect partners. Religious beliefs from childhood can seep into the relationship, and societal strictures in the form of roles and compensations can come to the fore. Oedipal issues emerge as deadness and even repulsion. In a number of workshops I have acted out the metaphor of "The Bee and the Flower" to describe this unhappy turn of events.

The Bee and the Flower

The flower wakes up one morning and decides there has been enough fooling around with all the bees in the meadow. It's time to settle down, so she gathers up her most unique and rare fragrance and sends it out to the bee that she's had her eye on. The bee has been happily gathering nectar and bizzzing all around the meadow, until one waft of the special scent lassoes him. "Bizzzzzttt!"

He hastens across the meadow, making happy little bee noises, "Bizz, bizz, bizz," until he reaches the flower. When he reaches her, she seems to have fragrance only for him. She wraps her petals around him and he is a happy little bee, "Bizzzzzzzz, bizzzzzzzz."

The bee and the flower marry and they are a happy couple. "Bizzt, bizzt, bizzt!"

But then something starts to change, and the flower no longer wafts out her amazing fragrance. Sometimes she even closes her petals with the bee on the outside. The bee droops more and more, "Bzzzs, bzzs, bzs." Sometimes he droops until he's just a shadow of his former self. Then he must choose whether to go back to the meadow looking for another flower, or droop away. If he decides to go back to the meadow and bizzes on his way, many times the flower will wake up and once again bring out her most exotic fragrance to draw the little bee back to her. The bee smells the special fragrance once more, "Bizzzzzt," and rushes, "Bizzzt, bizzzt, bizzzt," back to his flower. She greets him happily with petals wide open in welcome and he is a happy bee. "Bizzzzt!." But then sometimes the old fear of intimacy comes back, and the flower again begins to close up. The bee is once more left out in the cold, "Bizs," or begins to drift away. Sometimes there's a series of back and forths as the bee drifts away, "Bzs," only to be drawn back, "Bizzzzt." And so it goes. "Bizzzzt." "Bzs." "Bizzzzt." "Bzs." "Bizzzzt." "Bizs." Back and forth. It's a sad tale, but true.

A couple must be willing to commit to their sexual relationship, and to each other, over and over again to empower sex and bring it to the next, new beginning. In that way the fragrance is always shared and the "bizzzt" will always remain strong.

At the beginning of a relationship, we do everything for our partner's pleasure, but then it becomes a cursory effort at best. In the beginning, the woman is like, "Hey, where's that old love snake of mine?" Later, she gets crow's feet from scrunching up her face and saying, "You want me to suck on your whaaaat?!!!!"

Advice from the Old Sergeant

When I worked as a civilian psychologist for the Navy and Marine drug rehabilitation centre in San Diego back in the seventies, there was one young staff sergeant who worked on our floor as a counsellor. One day he was talking to his superior, an old staff sergeant, about his wife's reluctance to engage in sex. The older man listened to him awhile, and then suggested that he take his wife out on a date on Saturday night and get a baby sitter for the kids. He suggested dinner and dancing or whatever they liked to do, but that when they got home he would simply proceed to hold his wife with no overtures toward sex. Sunday would be the kids' day and the rest of the week they would both be quite busy and tired. But on the following Saturday he was to once again take his wife out for a nice dinner.

After the first Saturday night, the young sergeant announced that they'd both had a really good time. He reported how surprised his wife was that he had not made any sexual overtures or had any sexual expectations. The older man smiled and told him he'd done well. He told him to just follow his instruction the following week and let things take their course.

The following Monday, the young sergeant announced with a big smile on his face, "I just enjoyed the evening without thinking about what was coming next or having any expectations. We had barely sent the babysitter off when my wife started tearing off my clothes."

A man reading this last section has probably filed a bit of wisdom away for himself, while his wife is going, "Duh?"

Why are women always doing that?

Ladies, while there is some advantage to "quickies," you may want to teach your man the value of delayed gratification. If you succeed, you'll both be pleased with the results.

Male Psychology

Ladies, I am about to tell you the secrets of a man's mind. You will discover that, unless you been quite wounded or totally caught up in yourself, you will have a natural knowing about what I'm about to share with you. So now, if you have a minute, I will tell you all there is to know about male psychology.

First of all, as the old joke puts it, God gave men only enough blood to run one head at a time. This is depicted by the T-shirts you used to see couples wear at the mall, where the woman had a T-shirt that read "I'M WITH STUPID" with an arrow pointing next to her where her husband was wearing a T-shirt that said "STUPID." I prefer the T-shirt my best mate in the U.K. proudly wears, which reads "I'm with stupid" and the arrow is pointing down.

Ladies, while you were learning to play house and role play relationships as a child, you got a lot of practice in the key aspect of life – namely, relationships. While you were practicing for life and partnership, we boys were out playing army, sports and video games, which gave us a lot of practice in...well... army, sports and video games. So, for better or worse, you, as the woman, are both the leader and educator in regard to relationships, communication and sex.

Good Luck!

I'm sure you've heard man's motto:

I'M A MAN.
I CAN CHANGE.
IF I HAVE TO.
I GUESS.

So, ladies, here it is—all the salient facts about men are about to be revealed. As you attempt to educate us, you had better know who and what you are up against. First of all, remember to be gentle with us, as we are the more fragile vessels. Actually, research on babies shows that boy babies are much more sensitive than girl babies. This is encultured out of us early on so we are ready to meet the world as men and not as "wusses."

Dissociation

All of us are vastly dissociated. If our true state is Oneness, then we have cut off Heaven Itself from our awareness, as well as the love that makes us all one. Needless to say, we have cut off more than we are aware of. Joining in intimacy helps us find our way back to Oneness, step by step.

At a more down to earth level, when it comes to dissociation of emotions in relationships, men seem to have cornered the market. In a talk show recently, a psychiatrist interviewing a woman got this response regarding men. "Men have three emotions: angry, hungry and horny."

The more dissociated a man becomes, the more he turns to sex in order to feel anything. Sex can then be used to motivate him to regain his whole heart.

Dissociation is a defence that cuts off unwanted emotion and anything we find overwhelming, whether it be too positive or too negative. Love gives us the courage to open the many doors in our heart and mind that we have closed, making us more available to love and relatedness. The more dissociated we are, the less we like to be touched. Yet touching and feeling emotion are two of the ways reclaim our heart and create partnership. Without the ability to feel, there is no ability to receive.

As the guide for your man, it is important that you do not become indulgent about feeling your emotions or getting your needs met. Usually the extent one partner is hysterical or indulgent is the extent to which the other partner is dissociated. Both are actually avoiding the real emotion as much as possible. The hysteric feels lots of emotion, but uses that to disguise the fact that she is avoiding the real emotion at the heart of the issue. Indulgence can be used to avoid emotion in the same way. Indulgence attempts to get a need met, but avoids the emotion which, if addressed and healed, would free us of the need. So, as the woman, if you stay in integrity with your emotions, you will naturally entice the man back into his heart. Besides the inspiration and modelling this provides, it also helps you assume your place of natural authority and healing.

If you help a man find his heart, he will help you realize your amazing potential in sex. Sex between a man who has left his heart behind and a woman who has left her body is a real shame. It doesn't leave much to connect with.

Men as Heroes

Boys are raised to be heroes. This focuses our attention and gives us our reason for being. We want to show our love and courage. We want to prove our mettle as a man. The movie that depicts this element of male psychology best is Rocky I. Now, a woman watching that movie sees two men in the ring knocking the ever-loving glory out of each other. She sees them bloodied and battered and wonders, "What is that all about? What a waste." A guy comes out of the same movie brushing moisture off his face. He is touched and inspired, thinking "Rocky went toe to toe with the champ. He didn't back down. He gave as good as he got. Hey, what's going on with my eyes? Must be an allergy."

Ladies, if you don't understand this hero aspect of guys, you don't "get" what guys are all about. Now, besides the fact that the extent to which you understand your man will be the same extent he understands you, there is another, more powerful factor that works in your favour in regard to a man. He wants to be *your* hero. Everything he does, whether either of you are aware of it or not, he does for you. He will give his all for you.

In e. e. cummings' *six non-lectures*, he rendered this in a stunning way. He spoke of being up on a tightrope, high above the crowd, balancing on three chairs, one atop the other. The three chairs are the three facts of his existence. "I am a man. I am a poet. And I am a failure. A man, a poet and a failure must proceed." He speaks of the crowd below, applauding

24

because they don't understand, but that "your upturned face" sees and recognizes what he is doing and what he is giving, and that is all the recognition he needs. A man who is a poet and a failure doesn't stop, doesn't give up and is always willing to break himself open to move forward. A man feels that he can never be as good as his greatest ideals. No matter how many goals he reaches, his highest goals still measure him a failure against them. Yet his love carries him forward, and gives birth to new vision. It is a goal too far to reach, an impossible dream, born of love. That is why "The Impossible Dream" is the man's anthem.

In western literature, what delineates the tragic hero from the hero is not whether he lives or dies. What makes a hero tragic is that no one understands him, who he is, what he gives. This is why at the end of the fight, when Rocky raises himself bloodied and beaten from the mat, he cries out "Adrienne! Adrienne! Adrienne!" He's looking for her. It's she he needs to be seen by. At the deepest level, Rocky did it, not just for himself, but for her. She had told him she wasn't coming to the fight because she couldn't stand to see him hurt. But at the very end she was there to hear him call her name and she ran to him. The champ, who is also bloodied and battered, had his arm raised in victory, but Rocky's triumph was not just for Adrienne, it was Adrienne.

A man may be a great success and hero at work, but if he's not a success with his wife, he does not feel successful. I have seen many men who were heroes at work or in life, but had failed with their wives. The essential feeling in those men's lives was that they were failures. So whether you know it or not, or whether you understand it or not, your man is doing what he is doing for your eyes only.

The exception to this principle occurs if the man has become too independent, and thus is dissociated. This trap does not bode well for a healthy and happy relationship. The average couple has about ten thousand problems to heal before they reach balance and partnership in the relationship. This means going beyond both The Power Struggle and Dead Zone stages. While my wife and I went through all ten thousand steps, having done it through the long path of research, I would like to show you some shortcuts.

Taking Your Place

For a relationship to succeed, a woman must *take her place*. A woman is naturally the director, educator and leader in regard to intimacy, emotions, communication and sex. This is her function in the relationship. Without the woman taking her place and committing to equality, the relationship is rudderless. A man left to his own devices is not a pretty sight. He will be Don Quixote with his helmet askew, off fighting windmills or going on another useless crusade. If a woman has needs from her childhood that were not met by her father, and she tries to get them met now through her independent partner, she will be acting against her own interests. She may be wanting her man to be independent in an attempt to recreate her childhood and somehow finally get those little girl needs met, but the woman in her will be hating her man's independent behaviour. This is because, as a man becomes more and more independent, he first becomes dissociated, then he becomes a cad, and then a bastard.

The Quarterback

As the woman, you are meant to be the quarterback on the team. You call the plays. You direct the process. The only thing better than you taking your position as the quarterback is when you are so attuned that you let the "Coach" call the plays. This spiritual dimension adds power and stability to your relationship. As *A Course in Miracles* states from the November 12, 1966 section of the original text:

"God's power is forever on the side of His host, [that's you] for it protects ONLY the peace in which He dwells."

God will support you as the quarterback, keeping you in peace. Your peace is your confidence, and your confidence is your success. The Coach is always sending in a play that will allow you to be peaceful and conflict free. If you are a weak quarterback, avoiding your authority, the team will fail. You must take your place. And it is nice to know that you are being looked after from within by Heaven, and that Divine love can be present as a dimension of your relationship. As you listen to the Coach within, you will become better at coaching your husband. If you are not listening to inspiration you will not inspire him.

To take your place as the natural director and educator in the relationship is to value your relationship more than being right, getting your way and indulging your needs—all ways your fear holds your partner hostage. If you take your place you will find that you naturally direct your partner in a way that works well for both of you. If you direct gracefully, you will find a grateful partner. If you attempt to control, it will only lead to power struggle. A quarterback or a director does not control, they inspire and guide. Or, if they have another style, they give excellence and ask for it in return.

Equality

It is crucial that you pay attention to the level of *equality* in your relationship, because if it goes out of kilter you will have either a fight or deadness on your hands. If the relationship is imbalanced, and therefore not equal, then both your relationship and the sex in it will be unsatisfying. Achieving balance in a relationship establishes the intimacy and the confidence that was missing. Simply be on the lookout for times when you or your partner no longer seem to be equals, and recommit to equality until you reach a place where you are both at a higher level. This goes beyond the fifty/fifty range, where you first achieve balance. It ratchets you up into the higher levels of both stability and creativity in the relationship, such as 60/60 or 80/80, etc. If you want equality with all your heart, it will be yours.

Equality brings peace, and out of peace comes love, abundance, joy and every good thing. Remember, inspiration waits upon an open mind. The Coach's power is forever on your side. Sex can be used to re-establish equality, especially if it comes from generosity that surpasses the usual parameters of your relating.

If your old pain, indulgence, needs, righteousness and competition are more important to you than your partner and your relationship, everyone will suffer for it. When I worked as a marriage counsellor it became evident to me that if a woman is willing to take her place, accept her function and stay in emotional integrity, then, in spite of the challenges she and her partner face, the issues will unfold and be transformed as necessary for them to have a happy and powerful relationship. If the woman embraces equality she will have both the authority and the attractiveness to lead the relationship.

An example of lack of emotional integrity is when you push your partner to do something or try to get him to change. It is always when you are unwilling to change or take a step forward yourself that you do this. There is an economical principle in relationships that helps to bring about partnership: When one person truly takes a step forward, both partners get the benefit. A man's favourite form of growth is to have his partner take the step for him.

If your man is frustrated about being your hero because you won't let yourself be reached or helped, then you are driving him away. This usually is a form of passive-aggression, which will have disastrous long term repercussions. If you do this enough, he will look to be someone else's hero or, if he stays faithful, he will put his energy toward being a hero at work and you will become a work widow. If you understand what a relationship is all about, you will understand that it is your best chance for happiness and the fastest form of personal and spiritual growth. If you understand your man and are not making the relationship "all about you," then you will understand how easy it is to manage and motivate him. When you find him too stubborn, it reflects your hidden unwillingness to change. Just like a quarterback, your friendship and bondedness with him will imbue you with natural charisma and leadership. And, of course, there is also your allure, which is a cut above what quarterbacks have to influence and inspire their players. This allure will naturally be helpful unless you remain dependent instead of equal, and thus lose your attractiveness.

Motivating Your Man

Now we come to the topic of motivating your man. A natural part of motivating your man is knowing how important it is to both recognize him and let him know when he gets it right. When he's not getting it right, think of humour as the best way to let him know. Your recognition of him teaches him how to recognize and appreciate you. When it comes to motivation, you don't have to be a rocket scientist to figure out how to motivate a man. What every hero enjoys most is his beloved recognizing and rewarding him. And, how would he best like to be rewarded? Duh!

When I was courting my wife I sent her a card with picture of a blond fifties mom in her housedress and apron, washing dishes with her blond, blue-eyed daughter who was wearing a similar outfit. The little girl was looking up at the mom saying, "Mom, is it true that men only have sex on their minds?" And the mom was smiling down at the daughter saying, "Dear, men don't have minds."

Misuse

Ladies, if you have withheld sex as a weapon, or misused it as a form of manipulation, you have lost one of the greatest motivators and reinforcers there is for a man, and you will pay for it accordingly. Every fight is a pissing contest against the wind. Everybody loses and nobody stays dry. But, if you commit to using sex in a true way, it may not be too late. Another helpful step is to turn the mistake over to your higher mind for undoing, and let it be in charge of your sex life. Try it. You might be surprised how easy and effective it is.

Mr. Fix-it

Besides wanting to be the hero, the second major dynamic of male psychology is that of a "Mr. Fix-it." Sometimes this is helpful, and sometimes it will require all your patience. At some point your man will turn his desire to fix things, whether it be to fix problems, cars or household objects, toward you. So that when you are feeling bad or complaining about something, the hero joins with "Mr. Fix-it" and comes to save the day. He doesn't understand that *your purpose in expressing your pain is to receive love*. He is not seeing your obvious need for love because of his driving need to help. Give him a clue about this process, because until you do, he will be clueless. And you can't fault the guy if the thing that always works for him to make things better, namely sex, is his first thought for a solution. He doesn't know that if *you are loved* you will fix yourself, fix him and fix dinner.

His being a "Mr. Fix-It" is also one explanation for his fascination with sex. He looks at "the crack" and the first thing into his mind is, "Oh, no! Not 'the crack' again. I thought I fixed that! I guess I'm going to have to get the old glue gun out and fix it one more time!" Having something cracked like that is just too much of a temptation for Mr. Fix-it.

Remember he is not just from a different country; he is from a different planet. Educate him. Show him how to do right by you. He wants to learn. He wants to be your hero. You are the most important thing there is to him, even if he doesn't know it yet. If he doesn't know it yet, then the relationship is out of balance and you had best commit to equality with all your heart. Anything you want with all your heart, you will create. If your man stays independent, it's only a matter of time before someone gets victimized, namely you. If you are not his equal, you will not be able to educate or guide him. And if you are being dragged around by an independent man, look out. Remember—he wants to be your hero.

Ladies, your relationship is not all about you. If you don't learn this, I do not have much hope for your relationship or your happiness. If you make your relationship be about proving your specialness or getting your needs met, you won't be able to help your partner. That behaviour hijacks the relationship, and you will pay the price for it by seeing your man, your relationship and yourself fail, in that order. You can run from your failure in relationships through dissociation or by starting other relationships, but you can't hide. These failures build up as patterns. Guys do not know much about emotions, so it is easy for them to be emotionally indulgent or selfish in relationships without quite realizing it...but you are making the bed that you will sleep in. If he is indulgent in regard to his anger, then you must show him a better way. Teach him to not be afraid to feel and to share the deeper emotion that anger is always hiding.

What Sex Is All About

Sex is an aspect of communication. As such, it can be used to make a bridge to your partner. Take a moment to examine what you have been communicating to him through sex. If you don't like the message you have been giving your partner, then you can change it. If you are not communicating love, you are working against yourself. You can not escape doing to yourself what you do to others, especially significant others. How you are communicating in general will show you your subconscious patterns in sex. Take a moment to reflect upon what and how you are communicating to your partner.

Projection

The principle of projection is at work in your relationship. Knowing this can be very helpful because it lets you know what unconscious issues have been holding you back from having love and success. Seeing what problems you have hidden away can be very helpful in freeing you from emotional blocks and buried self-judgment.

What are your three major complaints about your partner?

1. ....

2 ....

3 ....

Next, list your complaints about your partner in regard to communication:

1 ....

2 ....

3 ....

Now, ladies, put on your big girl panties and get ready for this: Whatever you have been complaining about in regard to your partner, you have been doing also. It may not look like you are doing it. You may have hidden it under compensations or good make-up. But if your partner is doing it flagrantly, enough for you to complain about it out loud or just inside yourself, then you have the same self-concept inside you. Whether you compensate for it entirely or act it out from time to time, *you still torture yourself about it*. Once you recognize this, there is only one more step to take to free both of you from this issue. Do you want to keep torturing yourself about these self-concepts, or do you want to give up the torture chamber within to go help your partner? If you decide to help, imagine yourself giving the torture chamber to your higher mind to dismantle. See yourself leaving it behind so you can embrace your partner. This dissolves your self-concepts as well as his, and moves you beyond this troublesome behaviour to a new level of partnership.

Unless a man is very independent, he has learned not to communicate his complaints about what is not working for him about your relationship. A joke I heard in Taiwan illustrates this. A woman went to a fortune teller and asked with exasperation, "When will men finally share what they are feeling?" The fortune teller studied his crystal ball and replied, "On New Year's Day all of the men of the world will tell women what they are really feeling. And five minutes later, all of the women will be very unhappy."

If you're trying to get your man to talk so that you can gain reassurance from him, simply ask him for it. Don't ask him questions that drive him crazy, like, "Does this dress make me look fat?" A guy usually doesn't know how to communicate about things like that without getting himself into big trouble, so he'd rather not say anything. And, unless he is quite adroit, his replies *will not* reassure you anyway.

If you wish to know what his unspoken complaints toward you are, listen to the complaints he has about everything else and extrapolate them to you. Any communication from him about other situations or people is a symbolic metaphor for what he is subconsciously communicating to you, often without even knowing it. For instance, if he complains to you that his boss is dictatorial and doesn't really care about those working under him, he's really talking about you. The best thing you can do is heal this on your own without attacking him for his feelings. His feelings aren't right or wrong. They are right for him. Yet, any upset feeling is not the final truth. That is why feelings can be changed.

If you have not been modelling transformational communication or encouraging your man to communicate, you have probably been afraid to hear what he has to say. Most men feel emotionally bullied or blackmailed by their partners, so they have given up on communication. They see nothing positive in attempting to communicate because, for the most part, they see communication misused. Your man doesn't know how to use communication to bridge to you. If you were really interested, he'd be doing it already. Too many times, when he's tried to say something, he's ended up doing the "cowboy dance" in the face of your verbal six-guns. Many men feel that their wife "can dish it out, but can't take it." If you can give him a clue, so he knows what will work, then he can be your hero. If you spell out what, as a woman, you want, he will be eternally grateful, because then he sees what is being asked of him and he has a chance to get it right. Most guys simply feel at a loss as to what women want. Spell it out for him. What seems obvious to you is obtuse to him.

Most men I know hate it when their wives want to communicate with them. They go over to the closet, get the paint can and brush out, paint a target on themselves and say, "OK, dear, what is it you want to talk about?"

Another thing that drives men crazy is when their partner expects them to mind read in order to know what she is feeling, and why. If you can spell out, in plain language, exactly what you want your man to do, he has a fair to middling chance of success. If you expect him to read your mind, even if he succeeds, it won't satisfy you, because your needs can't be fulfilled simply by having someone meet your demands. Needs fall away when you let go of the control and independence that are hiding underneath the needs, to attain a deeper level of bonding.

A man found a genie's lamp, rubbed it and produced the genie. The genie said, "Let me get one thing straight. You only get one wish, not three, in spite of what you heard. And if it is too hard, than you have to make another wish."

The man said, "I always wanted to go to Hawaii, but I'm afraid to fly. Can you make me a highway to Hawaii?"

The genie said, "That comes under the category of too hard. Choose something else."

The man said, "Well, I always wanted to understand women. Can you help me understand women?"

The genie replied, "Do you want a two lane or a four lane highway?"

Most men's ability to sustain deep emotional communication is not very long. If you want to succeed in your communication, I would suggest no serious communication after 9 p.m., or he will start to fall asleep pretty quickly.

The Essence of Sex

Sex is the very essence of life. It is a way to bring us together in love. Done right, it's the closest thing to the experience of Heaven that we know. Yet, sex, divorced from love, while still heady, is merely "getting your oil changed" or a little "jiggy-jiggy." When sex is a function of love, it is the stuff of legends. This is evidenced by the fact that we remember those times when great sex with love occurred.

If you had a heartbreak in an early relationship, it could have broken the connection between your heart and your genitals. This sets up a pattern of victimization, independence or both, which has devalued your connection between love and sex. As a result, sex becomes a goal in and of itself instead of being a means to a goal, like communication. When this occurs, sex loses its real meaning and it takes on the meaning we assign to it, which is usually a lot less than is possible. Having broken our hearts because our needs and desires for specialness weren't met, we gained some control over the power of sex in our lives by disconnecting our "ding-dongs" and "twinkies" from our heart. We sought to make it less painful, but in so doing, we made it less intimate, meaningful and purposeful.

Sex has the power to transform us, especially when true intimacy occurs. It is not by accident that sex, death and transformation all belong together in the eighth astrological house. The French, in their inimitable style, call sex "la petite mort," or the little death. In transformation we die to what we were, and become more of ourselves. In sex, if there is real contact, the same change can occur, moving us not only closer together but also forward in a positive flow. If sex is shared as an act of love, both our vitality and peace increase from our "slippery celebrations."

Sexual energy generates life energy. I remember the last month before my doctoral dissertation was due, and I was pulling weeks of all-nighters. By two in the morning, I would be exhausted and "coffeeied-out." I had done push-ups to wake myself up so many times that it was only working for five minute stretches. Then I thought of my collection of nude magazines. Paging through these gave me enough energy for two hours of continuous work. By four a.m. I was exhausted again but I knew what would work. My thanks to all the ladies who supported me in getting my dissertation finished! Sexual energy can be used to awaken you both literally and figuratively.

A Significant Discovery

About a dozen years ago my wife and I gave a workshop entitled, "Rewriting Your Life Script." As the workshop unfolded, I found that people began dealing with their sexual issues, opening and clearing self-defeating subconscious and unconscious patterns in sex. What became apparent was that these sexual problems reflected corresponding life problems, and that there was a direct correlation between sexual issues and life issues.

About seven years ago, as I was conducting another ten day workshop, sexual issues once again became the main theme of the workshop. Once more it became obvious that sexual patterns directly reflect life patterns. Transforming patterns in sex, the symbol representing life, has the power to change lives. That sexual patterns correlate with life patterns is a principle that has been shown to me time and time again since then. It actually is one of the principles of hypnosis: If you assign something (a situation, an emotion, an addiction, a compulsion, etc.) a symbol, and then change the symbol, it has the effect of changing what it symbolized. In regard to sex being a symbol for life, I discovered there was already a natural correlation between the two. This means that if you change your sex patterns you can change your life patterns. This can save a lot of time in healing.

The Naturalness of Sex

Sex is a natural function of the body. Yet, the ego, seeing the power that sex has to generate real contact and flow, immediately sets out to sabotage its power through guilt and shame. This is especially true of religious guilt and shame used by others to control us. In the same way, we use guilt in an attempt to control ourselves, because we are afraid we might go sex crazy. This is self-defeating, because we cannot stand that feeling of guilt and shame, and therefore we dissociate even more. The more our dissociation increases, the more our sex life dies—or we increase the wildness in sex to allow us to be able to feel excitement in spite of the dissociation. It reinforces the very thing we are afraid of. These are defences that fit the ego agenda, because they strengthen the ego. Think of sex in fundamentally the same way you think about eating or sleeping—it's natural. Shame and guilt are traps the ego uses to stop the transformative power of sex, which would lead to a level of love and joining that becomes mystical.

The Body

The body is a vehicle of learning and communication. Everything we do is a form of communication to significant others. Everything we don't do also communicates to them. When we are not communicating love and friendship with our body, the body becomes a tool to gain control. Whether we do this through our health (i.e. through illness or injury), or sex (to dominate or gain the upper hand), we will use it to attack another, sometimes by attacking ourself.

Our Sexual Energy Centres

Our sexual energy comes from our first two chakras, or energy centres of the body. The first chakra, located at the base of the spine, is the energy centre that reflects our vitality. This vitality is life generating and can be used for sexual energy. The second chakra is the energy centre located three inches below our navel, and it is both the self-image chakra as well as a second sexual chakra. It reflects how we think of ourselves. Given the amount of self-attack rampant in the world, it is no wonder that the second chakra tends to be our most damaged chakra, which leaves our sexuality damaged also. It guarantees that we use sex to try to build ourselves up, but it also sets us up to be let down, because it is an attempt to use something outside us to build ourselves up

You can think of the energy in these chakras as a natural creative force. You can use this creative force for sex and experience pleasure as a result. Some people use sex for clearing their mind or simply to help themselves feel better momentarily. This sexual energy is meant to be used for love, joining, success, healing, service, health, celebration and even miracles. Off on a business trip, a businessman might think twice about frittering his sexual energy away through casual sex if he knew he could use it to build his business instead. We could all have another think about what we want to build with our sexual energy.

Temptation

Most of us realize that when we are tempted by someone outside our relationship it is because of the attraction towards something that is missing in our relationship. If we are attracted to another but still turn our sexual energy toward our partner, something paradoxical occurs. The quality that is missing develops in our partner within a two week period. I've seen this occur countless times for people in both personal and professional situations.

When I was young, foolish and single I did a lot of personal research in temptation. Because I hadn't found a way through the Dead Zone Stage of relationships, I had given up on monogamy. Once I began to date a number of women at the same time, I thought that the purpose of temptation was to fall for it. While I dated many lovely women, deadness stayed smotheringly near. Then one day, simply as an act of research, I formed a question: "I wonder what would happen if I didn't fall for this temptation?" As a result of this question, I enjoyed the new friendship, but kept my sexual energy focused on my main girlfriend. As a result, in about ten days, my girlfriend developed a quality I never thought she'd acquire, one that the other woman I was tempted with had. Then, in the interest of science, I began to test this idea out with the myriad of temptations that came my way. The same happy result occurred time after time. As I kept my energy focused on my girlfriend and simply enjoyed friendship with the other woman, my main girlfriend surprisingly began to develop the very quality I had been tempted with outside the relationship.

I once had a Japanese student who wrote a letter of profound thanks for teaching him this principle because his wife's bra size had gone up a couple of sizes that year as a result of his focusing his energy towards her. Let me remind you, though, that I am not really talking about the form that you are attracted to, but about the quality you imagine that you would get from the form, or, in this case, that the size would give you. My student must have experienced the quality that he thought the extra size would give him, as well as the size, to be so grateful.

The Creative Power of Sexual Energy

Sexual energy can be used in a many ways. You can use the creative power of sexual energy to deepen the love with your partner. You can use sex to build your health in the same way. Sexual energy could be used to improve your vitality by using your mind to raise that energy up through your body, adding to your overall well being. You could even take it to specific problems areas to increase your healing energy. I have received my doctor's advice on this very topic. My doctor came into the examining room the other day, shook his head and said, "Chuck, you have to stop masturbating!"

And I said, "What? Why?"

And he said, "So I can examine you!"

To emphasize this point, my older sister sent me a birthday card that expressed this very sentiment.

The front of the card said:

"I read somewhere that if a man has a hundred orgasms a year, it will lessen his chances of having a heart attack."

And on the inside was:

"In other words, your life is pretty much In your own hands."

Sexual energy can be used to build your life in any way you choose. You can think of sexual energy as money. Where and how would you like to invest it? To invest it toward your partner as an act of love has the power to move you and your partner forward. If you committed to the next step in your relationship, or simply committed to your partner, it would naturally bring you both to the next step. The bonding that would then occur would not only bring you closer and make your relationship evolve; it would also correspondingly move you forward in life, success, creativity, money, health, etc. The purpose of relationships is to help us become whole in what *A Course in Miracles* calls "a holy relationship." Then, as a result of the bonding that brings love and success with grace, it provides opportunities in which the joining is so profound that the dream falls away, and we experience that everything is connected, and Oneness is our true reality. This is what *A Course in Miracles* calls "the holy instant."

The holy instant, or experience of Oneness, can happen at anytime in a relationship and it can also occur during sex. My wife experienced this early in our relationship, during lovemaking. She describes it as a time when she had dropped all judgment on me and profoundly welcomed me within. As a result, she experienced the world and our bodies dropping away, and what is called a "Great Ray" was revealed. In this ray of clouds of pink and gold, Oneness extended forever, with both of us as part and parcel of it. She knew this all knowing, all loving light and bliss was God. During this communion, God, who knew her completely, was laughing at the joke that she believed she could be this little separate self. Lency could see that she, and I and everyone are all a part of God's light. Needless to say, this event profoundly changed her.

Men's Need, Women's Need

In a relationships course I taught in London in 1989, I described how women craved romance and felt loved as a result of the romance they received. All the women in the room sweetly acknowledged this point. Then I spoke of how, in a similar manner, men felt loved as a result of sex. The sweetness immediately dissolved into gloomy, incredulous looks. The women were completely downhearted that this was the level that men were operating on. I told them that this was actually the good news, because unless they were in a fight or judging sex, the care and feeding of their "couch potato" was relatively easy.

Motivating your man becomes rather simple. If you give a man all the sex he needs, he will give you all the romance you need. Of course, this is based on equality; if the man is independent, then he tends to see everything in terms of getting his needs met first, even if he is out to help. I heard a naughty story about how a man typically thinks of his needs first that illustrates this point.

A man and a woman were in a terrible car accident. While the man was unhurt, his wife was in a deep coma. The doctors conferred with him and said, "In our experience, there is one thing that can sometimes pull a person out of a coma."

The bereft husband replied to the doctors, "Anything! I'll do anything. Just let me know what it is."

The doctors said, "Well, we have discovered that oral sex can sometimes pull someone out of a coma."

"I'll do it," the determined husband said.

The doctors ushered the man into his wife's room, and then sat outside reading the instruments. After a while, all the alarms went off and they saw that the wife had flat-lined. As they were getting up to rush the revival equipment in, the husband came running out.

"What? What happened?" the doctors cried in unison.

"I don't know," her husband said. "I think she choked."

What's the Big Deal?

In a workshop in Switzerland about ten years ago, my wife talked to the women about men and sex. She was explaining about how important sex was for men. Again, there were looks of dismay from the women until finally she said, with slight exasperation, "Ladies, what's the big deal? It's only ten minutes of your time. If you could spend just ten minutes a day doing something that would make your husband totally happy, why wouldn't you do it?"

At that moment my buddy, who was sitting next to me, turned with a strange look on his face and said, "What am I going to do with the other five minutes?"

One female marriage counsellor in Hawaii has a way of describing how important sex is for a man. For him, having sex is like winning the lottery—it's that great. But his partner, being in her own world that revolves around her, isn't interested in even hearing about it. Of course, what I have been describing is how important sex is to a man when he first starts out in a relationship, and for the following few decades. When he is older, sex typically falls into balance. If, on the other hand, a man has been wounded a lot, he may try to dissociate and minimize sex, or he may dissociate but exaggerate its importance.

Sex and Independence

The extent to which a man is independent, and therefore dissociated, is the extent to which he will be attractive, because he seems to be "cool" and have it all together. Yet he will inadvertently break hearts, not necessarily because he wants to, but because, having dissociated from his own heart when it was broken, he will be unaware of the feelings of others. Also, and possibly more importantly, he will not want to be possessed by another. Those trying to capture him will naturally be disappointed, or even heartbroken. The independent man is actually resisting how he used to be when he was dependent and wanted to possess others. When he heals this by forgiving the one who broke his heart, or by integrating his old, needy behaviour that he had been judging, he can finally begin moving toward interdependence.

Mistakes in Sex

If a woman attempts to use sex as a weapon or tries to manipulate her man through sex, he will forego even his favourite pastime to avoid being manipulated. Yet, on the other hand, a man responds exceptionally well to "motivation and reward."

Your integrity is crucial if you wish to build the relationship and have it realize its potential as a vehicle for growth and happiness. Many times lack of fidelity in a relationship is a deal breaker. The intimacy and creativity that are the most soul-satisfying aspects of life are lost without integrity. Most people don't realize that lack of fidelity in a relationship blocks their ability to receive and enjoy. This can keep a relationship stuck, building a wedge between the partners. The ego pushes us into falling for temptations, and then it begins to plague us with guilt. The ego uses the first mistake against us, but the guilt and self-attack that follow just reinforce the first mistake, and make us feel even more separate. We end up making the same mistake over and over again, by missing opportunities for bridging because of the guilt. Do nothing that would hurt your partner. Do nothing that you wouldn't do if your partner were in the room.

The story of Goldie and Abie illustrates this point. Goldie and Abie were a young Jewish couple from Long Island. On their wedding day, Goldie asks Abie to leave a little something on the dresser for her every time they "did it."

"We're married! You want me to pay for sex?!" shouts Abie.

"Abie, if you love me, you'll leave a little something for me."

Abie finally concedes.

Forty-five years later, as Abie is retiring, he says to his wife, "Goldie, I'm sorry I didn't make much. We will only be able to afford a little cottage to retire in. "

Goldie smiles at Abie and says, "Abie, remember all that money you left for me on the dresser? We can retire and afford a real house."

Abie smacks himself on the forehead and says, "Wow! If I had known that I would have invested all my money in you!"

If you value your partner and the relationship, you'll keep investing in them. You'll keep working through the fights, deadness and your own fear of sex to keep your relationship and your sex life strong and viable. You won't use anything as an excuse not to move toward your partner.

Maturing

As men and women mature in a love relationship, sex and romance become less important as love is given more and more directly, rather than through the symbols of love. Yet both sex and romance can remain happy ways to join. The more a couple moves beyond the relationship stages of Power Struggle and Dead Zone, and make their way into the further reaches of Partnership, the spiritual element develops and the couple's minds turn toward God.

If you value your feminine aspect, you will value yourself. You will use your emotional intelligence to recognize what pain and dissociation has to be healed for your relationship to reach interdependence. You will heal the "wounded feminine" of the victim stage, and help your partner heal so that you both can be free. By valuing the feminine, you value joining over competition, and this balances the exaggerated independent masculine, bringing you both to partnership. People who do not pass through the Power Struggle and Dead Zone stages to reach the Partnership Stage are actually frightened to do so.

Things change in regard to sex. In my early twenties, all the young men I knew, including myself, were chasing women. By our thirties, it was the other way around.

A woman naturally grows into sex, and her desire for it, as the relationship unfolds, but if she has beaten off her man or held him hostage to sex, then she will face the natural consequences of her actions—loneliness. If, on the other hand, she acts truly, she will find her husband a willing partner and sex will be a natural acknowledgment of his love and her attractiveness. Sex will validate and confirm her as she gets older as much as she validated and confirmed her man when they were younger.

As a man approaches his golden years, he has less sex drive and may even start avoiding sex as issues of impotency loom up. This is less of an issue now with all of the virility pills that are available. But if a couple has had a good sex life, they will typically let it go easily, or they will continue to have a happy sex life long into their later years.

Helpful Hints

I. In the first stage of sex it's all happy times unless there is some infidelity. But in the second stage the relationship has progressed, and the woman wants to be known. She wants to be loved where she's at inside. Without coaching, this can be particularly challenging for a guy because in regard to sex, "it's all good" for him. With a few suggestions you can let him know that you want to be joined emotionally as well as sexually.

For a man this means intuiting and feeling where you are on an emotional level, so that while the lovemaking is progressing at a physical level, it's also proceeding at an emotional level. This provides the foundation for the powerful stages beyond this step. Many people are afraid to leave the Romance Stage of sex because they don't want to lose the high level of sexual energy. They feel they have lost something crucial in the second stage. But the second stage of sex is one in which we become much more mature. It is where we learn to join emotionally. If we do not learn the function of this stage of relationship, the relationship can start to die sexually and emotionally.

Your man may find that when he goes inside you emotionally during sex, you are not only a different age there, you may also be having different kinds of emotional experiences. Whatever you are experiencing, he can join you there and love you there. When he makes that level of contact, you really feel loved, and it will be pleasurable emotionally as well as physically.

II. When you are having sex with your partner, imagine pouring love into him. If you wish, you can alternate this with other energies, such as pleasure, tenderness, nurturing and playfulness. Once you have mastered this simple exercise, you can continue your exploration by sharing other energies. Simply remember "energy follows intention." See, feel, sense and choose what you want to share with your partner during sex. Notice your partner's response. This is a fun way to do research. Next, think of what your man craves. He may be craving your beauty, or your femininity. Touch him with this energy. Then pour it into him. As time goes on, you can also make love with him, and while you are pouring love into him, go back to ages when he may have been wounded, and pour love into him there. This will have the effect of reconnecting wires in his heart and mind, and sometimes even his body, if there was heartbreak that affected his health or his sexuality. Go back to the root where a certain need began and love him so profoundly that it dissolves his need in the present. Notice your success in this regard.

III. Make nothing more important than your connection with your partner. Let no bad feeling or any attachment be more important to you than he is. Your relationship can be your ticket Home if you give it that value.

How to Change the Life in Your Man Rather than the Man in Your Life

A man's favourite way to grow emotionally is to have his partner take the step forward for both of them. And because relationships have a great economy, when it is done truly and not as a form of competition, if one partner steps forward, both partners get the benefit. Now if you are complaining, "Why do I always have to be the one to do it!?" The answer is the same reason that he carries the big packages or moves the furniture (so reluctantly)—because he is typically the one better fitted for the job. This question always smacks of competition, which is very destructive in your relationship. Do you really want to continue down this path of the ego?

I have found that if you, as the woman, take a step in regard to healing or growth, to that same extent your partner will take a step forward also, maybe in money or success. This is the law of reciprocity, in which partners do the same thing equally, positively or negatively. An example would be if your partner were unfaithful, to that same extent you would have already stopped having faith in him. And where there is no trust, there is no love.

Now, ladies, besides stepping forward yourself, I would like to show you an even easier way to change your man. Remember, control hasn't worked, and if nagging or control actually could have done the trick, then you would have lessened the value of your man and your relationship in your own mind as you resorted to these tactics. If this is what you have done, it shows once again that you are just competing rather than partnering.

Remember, if your man fails you, it simply shows that you won the competition with him. If he seems to win over you, you are probably secretly proving that you are morally superior, and so you win the competition that way. Competition is destructive in a relationship. From it comes all power struggle and deadness. Only equality, reciprocity and generosity will give each of you what you want.

Listen Closely

The best time to generate a happy change in your man is while you are making love and have his rare, undivided attention. It's the same reason a man's IQ increases during sex. He's plugged into a genius. During sex, you can pour a gift into your man that would change him for the better.

Over the years, I found that in any situation we are in, we have a gift that would transform the situation. It may be hidden away under pain, grievances and guilt, but it is waiting to be opened and embraced. If you do this, the defences of pain, grievances and guilt quickly melt away. Let's say that your partner acts like "the south end of a north going mule." You would have brought a soul-level gift in (one you pledged to give to him even before this lifetime began) to help him to heal, and become more of his true, essential self. This gift may be truth, courage, willingness, love, happiness, right-mindedness, etc. Simply intuit what it is. Then go to the place in your mind where your gifts await you. See the door that is glowing amongst all the doors of potential gifts. Open this door, embrace the gift and share it with your partner energetically, especially during sex when he is wide open. You have many soul-level gifts that you brought in to help both him and your relationship, and sex is the perfect occasion to pass these gifts on to your partner. It helps *you* to share this gift with him. Everything you give to another, you give to yourself.

You can also ask Heaven, or whomever you are connected with at a spiritual level, for another gift for your partner. Simply receive this gift and share it with him energetically, especially during sex. Then notice the change that begins to occur in the next two weeks. You may even want to keep a small journal to record your experiences of giving Heaven's gifts to your partner. If you give these gifts during sex you will have the secondary benefit of your man happily following where you lead. Receiving Heaven's gift for both of you puts you in an even greater flow forward.

During sex you can also imagine going back to those times in your partners' life when he was most wounded, and at that point in time give him your gift and Heaven's gift, healing him and your relationship, layer by layer. In regard to your partner, you made a soul-level promise (before you were even born) that you would save his sorry ass and vice versa. Gift giving during sex is an easy way to do it. He will be a happy husband indeed. And when he is healed and his needs are met, then he will naturally fulfil yours. You will both be happy partners because you have been good partners.

The happiest moments in your life can be sexual moments if you use sex to join with your partner at even deeper levels. Deeper than a bodily connection, you can join mind to mind. This can help you realize you are one spirit, and experience the exquisite joy that goes with it.

As your relationship improves, it becomes a source of love, hope and inspiration to those around you.

Summary

Remember, if you make the relationship all about your specialness, you are sabotaging your best chance for happiness. Give up emotional indulgence for emotional intelligence. Take your natural function of leadership in regard to the relationship, emotions, growth and communication.

Be in integrity with your leadership function and you will have a willing learner.

Teach your man. Show him how to succeed with you. If he feels like he is failing with you, he will begin to give up on the relationship. Sex is a great way to motivate him. If you give him all the sex he wants (filled with gifts) he will follow you anywhere, and will give you all the love and romance you want. Let him be your hero. Together you will be a great team. Your relationship is your quickest path of growth, and it is your best chance for happiness. Sex is a real bridge builder in your relationship.

When he wants sex and you don't feel like it, just see it as an act of love rather than sex. If you see that giving yourself to him sexually is simply loving him, your sexual energy will kick in soon enough. Over all the years of our marriage, I have always appreciated my wife's Open Door Policy. Sex is a great way to come together in new levels of love and bonding. You can use sex not only as a bridge to each other but as a stairway to Heaven. Alternately, by accepting your sexual energy as creative energy, you can use it in all the other areas that it was meant for, including miracles.

Let sex be the sweet nectar it was meant to be to bring you and your partner together.

Lightning Source UK Ltd.
Milton Keynes UK
UKOW032117020513

210112UK00008B/173/P